# SEEDS OF LIGHT

Seeds of Light
Written by Jaskiran Singh
Print Edition

First Published in India in 2021
Inkfeathers Publishing
New Delhi 110095



ISBN 978-93-90882-17-5



www.inkfeathers.com

# SEEDS OF LIGHT

JASKIRAN SINGH

Inkfeathers Publishing

# CONTENTS

# Soil

Loved Ones,

The blue heart pushes forward each moment, for it has understood the power of receding.

For in time there is no love only the absence of it.

The great teardrop of the God- embedded in the ocean, the way our tears navigate themselves.

Understand this loved ones, in the present there is all, everything

all forms of Love rooted within you, but if you run after time... you will lose yourself, chasing the illusion

The abounding Love awaits you to escape

Free the mind that is the only way the Soul lives.

Escape before the addictions rule you.

Enraptured, what thoughts will you release?

Amused by your own captivity, what heart would you set free?

Imprisoned by your own mind, how will you mentor yourself and learn how it feels to fly?

# Root

The mantle shaken; disturbed in natural motion,

mirrors awaken, disarrayed are only thoughts,

plexus, stirring in craft of thine chest,

each beauty mark a point of rest,

an error in creation.

Pleading ghosts, wearily awaiting,

confirmation,

perfused spirits,

breakage, bandaged,

divinity worshipped.

For what am I but a piece

Seated and at once, dangling

Tying my soul with mimicking eyes

Failing myself to learn you

The spirit of love imprisoned

felon heart

charged by bondage

the power of self-will un-ordained

The clearest conscience, attempted the dirtiest crime

Tying my soul with mimicking eyes

For what am I but a subject of my own pride

Without an us, I would have remained nothing of me

“it is not love, stop pining to be worthy…”

Let your heart hear your prayers

Forget the felony of the ego

For when he asks, "what do you want from me?"

Repeat from the center of your heart…from the mind apart

I have been played, plucked, chosen for a lesson as harsh

blessed I am to have learned of my own worth

melody is endless…

harmony is true

my purity has renewed

I am worthy of Love

it is not you who I pine to love

but I, the lover I longed to love

hold, whole, impart

wisdom in camouflage

# Pain

Simply grand, the perfection we strive to achieve

Dismissing what we already are made to be

Struggling for sanity, peace, unity, familiarity

And here is where I am, completely, remaining, staying.

She has no title

She comes with no features

There is no her, or I

No secrecy

No deliberate fallacies

Imposing opinions

Conditioned love

Running of programs

Or breaking of trust

No branding, no propaganda

Rarely does this body sleep

Vibrating immensely, chasing nothing

There is no need

Romance knows no boundary

Impassioned Love directed by divinity

Nobody will write her will

For she never lived

Forever has slipped away

Eternity has arrived

Corroborate your soul, bury your lust, embed trust

# Truth

The candle fused,

She rests her head, as her thoughts spindle webs...

You aren't his

He is not yours

You'll make all the excuses in the world,

You'll dream of all places

To observe,

you'll wander, you'll fall, you'll touch,

you'll corrupt

all that is left is Blood

digitalized lust,

And what should you do with these veins of madly passionate love?

Serve.

fall onto your knees and pray

Oh…to your dismay the mind must obey

Divine Queen how your heart has been mistaken

How your pride has gone array,

How your face has aged a billion days, how your life won't be the same

How nature has changed

Speaking nothing of you,

mighty stars passing away

how you have stopped twinkling

What kind of love must it have been?

For you to have become grim

Falling across the sky, one wish at a time

How you remain at rest as the vastness sleeps

heed the understanding

Oh no, never, the pain of loss through pleasure is far too deep,

Unfathomable,

until you open your eyes

The moon too is no longer bright or white, you see nothing

Just yourself.

That is all, but even that, you do not know,

lost in your shadow

nothing found there

a crater or emptiness,

muscles of despair,

you cry and cry, until there is nothing left to weep, when can you close these sullen

eyes, sore and weak?

What should you do with all your contemplating?

Fall onto your knees

the moon is full,

all blood imbued,

you lost you,

having found the truth

# Emergence

I look back

Looking forward to see

you knowing it can't fall

through knowing I

couldn't be used

counting the
minutes, ticking
off my veins,
crippled by assault

here goes my chance
to fly my feet tracing
the ground lifting to
see sounds
hear movement
in stillness aloud
I see clearly
my arguing resound

tears swell in my eyes

dreams drown me in reality

I kept the tsunami in my being

as a mirror of my securities

and now it cripples me,

the Gift of life to be presented in one single moment,

and all I can do is sit here thinking of you…

Into the palms of death, far too vain

Rainbow bird, nectar's curse, flawless creature

Creation has made you the hardest to subdue

In the cocoon you knew,

The day of your catharsis would elevate the spirit,

the chastening of your wings leads you into captivity

and this is the moment you arrive Home,

emit your love butterfly

beautify those petals

remind us of the light

conceived before

the opened Womb

and now her color is jaded

# Love

Writing, not thinking

Feeling, non-believing

Trusting never knowing

breathing

the mindless dreaming

Imaginary not depicting,

Awakened meditating

Craving agony

Tasting bliss

Turning away from life's kiss,

Adorned, not by objects of desire,

You, the beholder ought to arise,

from the insight

Arise and be

Arise and love

Arise in love, to love, for love

create thyself to reach above

In the meeting of the eye

the mirror faces me

a direction where I can see- muse

strength clarifies needs- standing

in the collisions- punish me

What does it matter, from what do we empty?

faces twitching- bodies ticking- compulsions

break into the stars- mediums of infinite illusions-
they call

brilliance stains the internal state

convinced of black, as if there are days, as if there is
time

experiencing the light- heal me

inside the art- alive- touches of magic into my image

so that I may breathe- in the reality- reverence
abounding

angels call onto me- inside the colors of my eyes-
glistening

eyes cleanse the old

love anew

the message heard from life itself

Beautiful to be here

to be you

if I love myself- I truly love you

disguises observed- fights in movement-

gifted to serve- humbled hearts made to shield

delicacy in stillness

touches of magic into my image

Bow to the journey

to be renewed

back to Love- Back to you

These are your words- mi amor

You ponder on completion

set free already

the imprints of soul

pink imbued

infinite reflections- permeating revelations

the mirror speaks- listen

the heart whispers entangling words of love

Love interrupts- powerfully this time- I feel the urge to stand- I wanted to grab my things and storm away-

I know I will be followed-

I start to recite my poem aloud- and Love listens- healing my soul- warming what has been cold for as long as I could know-

Love touches my shoulders- easing my stiffness- melting my sharpness- I begin to allow- my words become refuge- let me love you-

heart fills with art- paintings of immaculate love-

I find my match in Love- I find myself in Love- the face of love becomes my reflection and joy takes sorrow- I store it in my locket- the sorrow that is to remind me again of the Love that truly does exist

# Tears

He had a name, given or to take…

Pining for a girl, she noticed, obscurity

Strange she thought, standing like an ambushed victim,

Certainly not as tall, interesting features, knuckles for a brawl

Lighting up the night

Smokey eyes, burning jaws

Being lucid he says, is my greatest flaw

towards the Sky, the stars watching;

cautionary shared connection becomes the beggars addiction

he rests in the furthest corner of the dark, lurking for the fallen,

impaled

she sees how convinced she is…that someday he will muster the strength to be walked beside again

lighten his name,

and maybe bring back the color in her face,

polarize pain and fate

in him she sees the iridescent shadow of the rainbow,

a parabolic smile

and he the shadow of her, concave

the craters of wounds

tarry, smitten, molding

imparity

# Illusion

aiming at shifting frames

standing within the celestial plane

invested without a gain

mission to believe- in faith- there is a timeless creed

dismantling delusions-debilitating convulsions-

falling into a symphony

Catch the Almighty

symbols of peace among the reckoning

intrusive and necessary

happenings with no restraint

the only restriction known to man- the mind-
collapsing in time

escalades inside-protective measure for shadow studiers

if there is love why do we refuse to serve?

conditional- suddenly a verb

if innocence is valuable- why then is it - on a platter to be served?

if the truth must be told- how is it that only lies are heard?

deep exhalations for the weight is indescribable- in segments- in waves- in words-in phrase-

why such a deep agony yet a porcelain face?

an emptiness to be dispelled in this heaven on Earth- converted in Hell

grievances to be settled- betrayers must meddle

flying away from fate

to be of purpose you must be paid

if stillness came at a cost- what price could you pay?

is prayer ever emptied of personal gain?

The frameless externality- the timeless
omnipresence

Unfolding before you

Coming undone in your arms

What a novelty you are

Your eyes shone

Your heart aglow

Holding me

Touching your soul

What a majestic sensation

The fingers of a pianist

Pressing your chest against chords in my torso

Enraptured

Subdued

You know I've known

Poured out onto your sacred plane

Answers in between cleavage

Whispering not for more

Enough is enough

You in your enlightened heart

Moving outward-reach for me

The parts of us we know, set aflame

Let the turn, form rise, sparkling

Ashes, love, scraps of your notation

Falling from my eyes

Tears putting out alchemy

What is this

When we know

Of only you not of me

Gambling our youthful mortal lives

Passion in your eyes, blazing like a gazillion Suns

I wonder why I am not yet overcome,

proscribed is your mind

protected by the Divine,

you have decided for me

disqualified, barely beginning to learn of love

let alone speak

hollow are my cheeks, disintegrating face

an infant, unable to assimilate

I reckon too, baptized through you

symmetry your middle name, a flawless hex

fooled is Evilness

articulate, immaculate, sharp and soft, the water too
has come to a halt,

the sound of your voice enough

eroding my solid heart, make a jaded fossil of me

store me someplace beneath your feet

for I may be touched again by Thee

# Self-Worth

She compares her worth, every time falling short,

She refuses to see all that is missing

Only Her acceptance of the honor,

For she is pure in all her actions and deed,

indoctrination at its finest,

She is the nurturer of all, yet, the bearer of the pain
from every fall,

What does she fail to see, whom is she yet to meet?

The love she once felt, still captured in her Soul,
spilling onto her wings…

Cocooned, she protects her wound,

Torn epiphanies,

citrus orchards

blue bruises

scratchy throats

misguided muses

helpless hands

lightweight hearts

heavy eyes

thousands of miles

empty insides

hungry souls

whispering willows

waned hope

Where did you go?

drunken mind

exposed spines

burnt in time

chilling cries

Why must you hide?

youthful cruelty

devilish pride

you let him inside

imparted whole

Celestial wretch

And yet,

They ask where you went.

She holds a space in her heart

earthy hurt is welcome

Swaying as she walks

Cradling her elusive pains

Singing to her brethren

Intelligent in the way she advances

Obstacle

gears for change

Genuinely

a woman is a true gift

once discarded

obsolete illicit

Planet of pearls

Remaining in luster

Resting on her head wrinkles of courage

A craft to eradicate, inject, do away with

The woman could never permit to dismiss

The same woman has been lost, targeted

Raised barely above a fiery pit

for beauty is those whom suffer inwardly

pose, click, filter, the blood cleaned from her wrists

fake it until you become it

advertise your body

next thing you know

you bargained your Soul

wagering war

planet of pearls

ashes of injustice, transformed

she is an obligation

the virgin burden

# Reflecting

Rejoice

before

me

beckons

the enamored mirror

hand of god

attuned to draw

miraculous inundations

the diabolical questions eroding

doubts forecasting

climate of clarity-

plumed, the soul tarnishing in violet streaks

festering in the heart of my shrine

blooming upon me

the newly becoming

the framework of a flower

a stem flickering

there was a moment when I felt I believed in her

she is intending to give birth- the portal has opened

she steps through to you

all curses removed- her flowers destined- they grew-
whether or not they knew

I find her sometimes in the emptiness of the garden-

whimpering

she dances in orbs- splendidly- ardently

a thorn in her tendon- a grimace- she does not bleed

her pain is opportunity - she fathoms now her
threshold

what was once a gestalt

now all the eye can see

beheld and infinite

a light is born

and from her the stems are nourished

she breathes into

life from the endless source

and from her follicle a dove cooes

strands glorifying what she is made of

only hope could know

from love she has been bestowed

# Realize

there is much to learn from the trees

untouchable- surrounded not smothered

tall enough to surrender to the Earth- grounded
enough to elevate

there is nothing to be sad about- upon a sea of
bladed grass- I feel the presence of your absence-
love

stores the unforgettable

leaves do not speak unless the breeze beckons

I am fond of listening

caressing what anguish offers

alone enough to be embraced

betrayed enough to entrust

solitude that bears answers

remain grounded to illicit truth

falsified enough- nothing to be kept

what is there to seek?

transient enough to be everlasting

# The Duplicate Truth

been waiting for some time

for this to be recognized

inside the quiet spaces of my mind- where the hollowness becomes shallower

I find the answers

what happens now

they ask for your number not your name

they ask for your address not your destination

they ask about your occupation not of your morals

they ask for your documentation not your mission

they ask about your associations not your intentions

they inquire of your goals but never your story

whom can you trust in a world as such

striving to create change in a place that holds onto
instead of refrains

what kind of change I ask myself can I possibly bring
in to this world who covers my face

when religion has taught injustice and the
government has enslaved

how can I pay my dues when I have been stripped of
my values?

whatever it takes- keep pushing replay- stand before
what you think you own and watch it be foreclosed

you think the music does not know?

you are being watched

you are already sold

there is a victory to be had- it cannot be seen- we speak in secrecy- the codes cannot be heard unless you

approach

you choose to hide under the products

you choose to whisk away- that is not why I came

the fight is brutal- it's my turn in the ring- it has been ever since

# Forgiveness

## Dense Hearts

plastic that melts into pure limerence

the body is becoming lighter- fluid

as change begins to tap on my shoulder

coiled barely above the fire

I look forward- pulled by my past- another clash-
swerve

the eyes go from pink to red

wings fluttering above I

to each their own constellation

as the spirit calls for us to realize

we may not notice what loss has incurred

we lest not think this way- for we are grounded in our honor

integrous

in observance of the moistened eyes there is a dove

inside treachery there is an unheard symphony

for that in high vibration will transmute disharmony

faith is needed- for what is on the ridge of the heart

runs through the veins

I felt my bones shivering- the sound of spirit bolsters me

pain has a choice to leave- filter it through- take upon yourself a life anew

prayers in poetry that drive into your mind

diversified

to carry your heart in mine

may be set free through love

multiple lives within one life

potentialities

marred in victim consciousness let what is meant to
be: release

# Evolution

With my eyes closed ever so loosely that the tightness of my lips becomes known… they are zipped until

Only the Truth can be told

I feel the Sun in my body, snowflakes crystallizing in my heart space

Melting into my Soul, a balance occurs, fluidity, nurture,

love endures, trust

stand, spirit says, though you may need to deplore, let that part of you die away, wistfully…

peacefully… trusting summer will bring winter

allow for the resonance within to allure your resting mind to an Awakening, you may be weak, it is only an idea

you may feel broken, this is nothing but an intended design

stars twinkling swimming past sockets of distress

this will fill my cup

mastered acquiesce

It was not just my body it was my light not only a moment of passion but a lifetime of delight

birthing symphony

a true divine collaboration unprecedented

there may not be another moment in time reaching heights

rescuing lows verbiage so gentle from the soul

it was not just my body but my aura you were given to hold

stored within itself if of course the nameless comes to claim

the same way they once came

I wanted you to know love

in its highest form percolating

and now the search has begun

for another place to worship another saint to guide another lifetime an angelic force entrusting what I know

resting in my beingness I wish you could know

I wish you could feel but perhaps this will never happen

I forgive you before you hurt me

before you collapsed into my frame- unapologetically

my face open to judgement

my heart closed in on pain

marking a territory- daggers throbbing

insulation for what I was keeping cold- I am brittle now

growing wiser- fragile upon this Earth- I feel her groans in my body, it was not just my body- but a pure mind

I am not just a body- to suffice desire not a source to feed from- slowly dimming the flame

so I allow enlarging your greatness- enforcing what you may have never known

the place within is not what you once knew departing, it was my light and you the darkness I shined

through- illuminating before you for you- expanding into her realm

The heart that loves is eternal

forever lasting

You have a presence, fearless, enamoring.

Hold your Affinity to Thy Self, Love.

And instead of being blinded by Light, Immerse,
Become ONE, let the seeds of

love plant and nourish

them from beneath

# Acceptance

The Queen is creating,

in a place, good, wonderful, beautiful and yet… in my soul I know I owe you an apology.

I keep choosing them over me… losing the identity to a crisis not belonging to me,

For a taste of empathy; a hand held must be felt

Dearest love, I have fallen so hard rising to the surface is the deepest torment, and like the tide I climb weeping… waving, wading, not for you, but for me, accept this dissipating apology.

I am deeply sorry.

You will not recognize me, let me warn you, my
honesty might leave you trembling…

But I urge myself to be courageous.

You walked away from me, my outreached hand

opened heart, portraying the shards

exposed Soul

this must be how it is meant to be

Light house within me

Swimming in recede,

Rumbling in Love, Enveloping Turbulence,

Aligning with my loving Moon... once again... a seed
of love...

The unraveling

You're almost complete, keep planting

Wilting in form, expanding in essence

The day you recognize

You are Me.

The purpose this anthology carries attempts to illustrate virtues of the light. We must become consciously aware and awaken to our fears, doubts, and the things that we hold onto that hinder us from shining our light.

Reflect without projection,

Practice compassion away from judgment

Make empathy your prayer

The Divine is your Guide

Simplify your way of life

Plant seeds of love, carry water as though it is light

let the pain transform into a blossoming this much,

to yourself, you deserve